Brian Webb & Peyton Skipwith

Edward Bawden

DESIGN

ACC ART BOOKS

Design Series format by Brian Webb
Design, Edward Bawden © 2016 Brian Webb & Peyton Skipwith

The works of Edward Bawden © The Edward Bawden Estate

World copyright reserved

ISBN 978-1-85149-839-0

British Library Cataloguing-in-Publication Data
A catalogue record for this book is available from the British Library.

ACC Art Books Ltd
Sandy Lane, Old Martlesham,
Woodbridge, Suffolk IP12 4SD, UK
Tel: 01394 389950 Fax: 01394 389999
Email: info@antique-acc.com

ACC Distribution
6 West 18th Street, Suite 4B,
New York, NY 10011, USA
Tel: 212 645 1111 Fax: 212 989 3205
Email: sales@antiquecc.com

www.antiquecollectorsclub.com

The cover and title page illustrations are reproduced from London A–Z,
published by Andre Deutsch, 1953.
Endpapers reproduced from The Arabs by R.B. Serjeant, a Puffin Picture book, 1947.
Opposite, stencilled illustration for A Catalogue of an Exhibition of Books
Printed at the Curwen Press, held at J&E Bumpus Ltd, booksellers, 1929.

Published by ACC Art Books Ltd, Woodbridge, England
Design by Webb & Webb Design Limited, London, England
Printed and bound in China

PORTRAIT.   **BAWDEN.**

A hand-coloured illustration from *Gallimaufry, A New Magazine of the Students of the RCA which Will Appear for this Once Only*, June 1925.

Design
Edward Bawden

Edward Bawden was one of twentieth-century Britain's most innovative graphic designers. Book illustrator, wallpaper, textile and poster designer, watercolourist, mural painter, teacher. His designs still resonate strongly with young designers more than a quarter-of-a-century after his death. Born in Braintree, Essex, the son of a Methodist ironmonger, he was addicted to drawing from an early age. From the Friends' School at Saffron Walden he progressed to Cambridge Art School, where he discovered old volumes of The Studio magazine and decided he would become an illustrator. Ambitious to get to London, he won a scholarship to the Royal College of Art; however, lacking the confidence to tackle the major disciplines of painting, sculpture and drawing, he opted for 'industrial design', a discipline consisting in those days chiefly of calligraphy. He was successful and enrolled in the Design School at South Kensington in September 1922, the same day as another scholarship boy – Eric Ravilious – who had come from Eastbourne Art School. It was a meeting of opposites, and an instant friendship was formed, which lasted until Ravilious's untimely death in 1942.

The Royal College of Art in the early '20s, under its recently appointed Principal, William Rothenstein, was just embarking on a golden period. In 1922 the Design School was still under the care of Robert Anning Bell, an Arts and Crafts polymath in the William Morris tradition – stained glass designer, sculptor, painter and illustrator and a Past-Master of the Art Workers' Guild. He retired the following year and was replaced by the mediaevalist, E.W. Tristram. Architecture – a compulsory subject for first-year students – was taught by Beresford Pite, another pillar of the Art Workers' Guild, and calligraphy by Edward Johnston. One of Rothenstein's most important innovations was to persuade the authorities to allow him, in addition to the regular staff, to employ artists and craftsmen

One of Bawden's earliest tile designs, and commercial commissions, for Poole Potteries, c1925. His last job for the Poole Carter Company was the design of a ceramic coat of arms in black and white mosaic for the High Commissioner's residence in Lagos, Nigeria in 1961.

on a part-time basis, as a result; Paul Nash joined the staff of the Design School in 1924. His work and example was to have a profound influence on several of the students, particularly Bawden, Ravilious and Enid Marx. Another part-time tutor was Harold Stabler, a partner in Carter, Stabler & Adams, the Poole Pottery, for whom Bawden was to design a series of pictorial tiles, while William Rothenstein's nephew, Oliver Simon, was a partner in the Curwen Press. Thus, all the influences and necessary contacts for his professional life fell into place at this most formative moment in his career.

Bawden's tiles quickly found favour among a discerning clientele, such as Rupert d'Oyly Carte, who incorporated a number of them into the bathroom decor of his Devonshire house, Coleton Fishacre, which Lutyens's former assistant Oswald Milne was building for him at the time. The house, complete with its Bawden tiles and extensive gardens, was acquired by the National Trust in 1982 as part of its Enterprise Neptune campaign to link the Devon coastal paths. Stabler also commissioned the booklet *Pottery Making at Poole*, which was printed at the Curwen Press. According to Oliver Simon, his initial meeting with Bawden was totally silent, but a rapport soon developed between the two men, and with Harold Curwen, and Bawden became the in-house artist for the Press. For the next few years he would work one day a week in the disused chapel in Plaistow, East London, drawing illustrations, decorative borders, swelled rules and other devices as required, and it was Harold Curwen who skilfully transcribed Bawden's linocut designs for pattern and wallpapers for lithographic printing. The influence of Nash at this period was crucial, not only as a watercolourist, but more particularly as a designer as, inspired by the example of his friend, Claude Lovat Fraser, he had also started designing pattern-papers for the Curwen Press. Nash went on in the next few years to design books and bookjackets as well as textiles. Designing, whether for papers or textiles, as Bawden was quick to discover, gave scope for the exploration of abstract pattern, which fed back strongly into his figurative work.

Bawden's earliest surviving project from his Royal College days is the twenty-two page illustrated manuscript, *General Guide to the Royal Botanic Gardens Kew Spring & Easter 1923*, with its elegant lettering, maps, vignettes and full-page illustrations. The innocent naivety of this work, coupled with Bawden's precocious powers of observation and command of detail, attracted the attention not only of his teachers but also of Frank Pick, who was in charge of publicity for the Underground Electric Railway, and hastily commissioned a poster for the 1924 British Empire Exhibition at Wembley. It was a daring commission and proved too big for the twenty-one-year-old Bawden to handle on his own; it eventually evolved into a collaboration between him and the more experienced Thomas Derrick, with Derrick creating a complex plan of the exhibition and Bawden filling in the detail in lively vignettes of football, picnics, merry-go-rounds, etc. giving full-rein to his youthful irreverence. In format, it owed a considerable debt to MacDonald Gill's 1914 *Wonderground Map of London Town*. This was swiftly followed by three more posters for the Underground: *Changing the Guard* and its partner *Hyde Park — The Stage of London*, plus one advertising the Natural History Museum. He also illustrated a series of press advertisements depicting such subjects as art galleries, museums and dancing, publicising the advantages of the Underground for ease of access and egress; *Dancing* ends with the injunction: ...Take your partners for the next dance, please", but, unlike Cinderella, be sure to catch the Undergound.' These, like *Pottery Making at Poole*, were also printed at the Curwen Press. Bawden had hit the ground running.

Throughout his life, Bawden remained excruciatingly shy, which, during his student days made him monosyllabic and unsociable; he evinced little or no interest in girls, music, sport, the cinema, or any of the other activities that formed an important part of out-of-hours college life. He would return alone every evening to work in the digs in Redcliffe Road on the borders of Chelsea and Fulham, which he shared with Ravilious, and it was here that he made his earliest copper engravings as well as his first linocut. He was later to describe how, one evening on his way home, he bought a piece of ordinary household linoleum and, with the aid of a pocket penknife, cut the image of a cow and printed it. By the end of the evening he said he had a small herd, which in due course evolved into *Tree and Cow*, one of his most popular wallpaper designs.

His biggest break, however, came in 1928 when he, Ravilious and Charles Mahoney, a fellow RCA student from the Painting School, were commissioned to paint murals for Morley College in South

London. Sir Joseph Duveen, grand dealer and patron, had recently underwritten the expense of Rex Whistler's mural, *The Expedition in Pursuit of Rare Meats*, in the Refreshment Room at the Tate Gallery on Millbank. Whistler had been a student at the Slade School and Rothenstein, ever active in promoting the Royal College, approached Duveen to see if he would consider supporting some RCA students in a similar project. Duveen agreed and along with Rothenstein and Charles Aitken, Director of the Tate, they selected Morley College as a suitable site. Morley had been founded as a College for Working Men and Women and had originally been housed within the complex of the Old Vic Theatre, but by this time it had acquired its own premises, in Westminster Bridge Road nearby. Bawden and Ravilious were given the task of decorating the Refreshment Room, while Mahoney was assigned the Assembly Hall; after discussions with Rothenstein and Duveen, the themes eventually decided upon were sixteenth-century drama for Bawden and Ravilious, and *The Pleasures of Life* for Mahoney. They were supplied with materials and paid a pound a day each for their work, and the completed murals were unveiled amid considerable fanfare on 6th February 1930 by Stanley Baldwin, the former and future Prime Minister. Thus, five weeks before his twenty-seventh birthday, Bawden's public reputation, and that of his friends, was firmly established. Sadly, Morley was reduced to rubble ten years later during the Blitz, but for Bawden it was the curtain-raiser on another strand of his career – mural painting – which he was to exploit most effectively during the decades following the Second War.

The reason that Bawden had lacked the confidence at Cambridge Art School to tackle the disciplines of painting and drawing as scholarship subjects was largely due to the fact that his teachers, while recognising his talent, could not understand his approach. They said his figures tended to lack substance – more 'Flat Stanley' than 'Billy Bunter' – being delineated by outline rather than the conventional shading. Given this, it is no surprise that the drawings in Edward Lear's *Books of Nonsense* were among his early sources of inspiration, and one of his contributions to the December 1923 issue of the Royal College of Art *Students' Magazine*, edited by Douglas Percy Bliss, was a Lear-like caricature *Cuculus Canorus Hunticus*. His distinctive style, coupled with his humour and unrestrained urge to create pattern, soon led to his work being in demand from publishers and advertising agents, quickly establishing his reputation with the

The editorial team: D.P. Bliss, Sam Heiman (later Hemming) and J.A. Betts, headpiece illustration and, opposite, *Cuculus Canorous Hunticus* 'The South Kensington Cuckoo', from the *RCA Students' Magazine* number 7, December 1923.

public. Apart from dust-jackets, the first book that he illustrated was a new edition of Robert Paltock's mid-eighteenth-century traveller's tale, *The Life and Adventures of Peter Wilkins*. Published jointly by J.M Dent and E.P Dutton of New York, the dust-jacket blurb proclaims *Peter Wilkins* has 'forty drawings in color and line by one of the most original illustrators of today giving an interpretation unique in technique and conception.' The most original illustrator was just twenty-five years old and the technique was that of engraved line and *pochoir*, the stencilling process for hand colouring that had been developed in France and exploited in England, especially by Harold Curwen, for the production of high-quality books in smallish print-runs. Another book lusciously illustrated in the same manner was *Adam and Evelyn at Kew*, published by Elkin, Mathews & Marrot in 1930, one of the last of its kind as the Wall Street Crash had decimated the print and fine book market, forcing even the Curwen Press to close down its stencilling studio.

Bawden, however, was not reliant on colour, he was at heart a black-and-white man, and throughout the thirties his line embellished advertisements, trade cards, prospectuses, menus and even a Romary's biscuit tin. He had a sure hand and a keen eye and his witty and incisive drawings for Shell, BP, Imperial Airways, Fortnum & Mason and Twinings continued to beguile the public, as did his illustrations for Faber's series of books by Ambrose Heath *Good Food, More Good Food, Good Savouries*, etc. His style was instantly recognisable, as was his humour; if any illustrator today had the temerity to submit drawings depicting flies, caterpillars and wasps to embellish the pages of a cookery book they would be laughed out of court, but our forebears were less squeamish about such things. The original 'Ambrose Heaths' are not only highly prized by collectors, they still get reprinted from time to time, as much for their illustrations as for their recipes. The Shell advertisements with their punning captions based on unusual place names such as *Coton-in-the-Clay but Shell in the Tank, Leigh-on-the-Solent but Shell on the Road,* and *Ashby-de-la-Zouch but Shell sur la Route,* were created in collaboration with John Betjeman: among Bawden's classic drawings for these are Wormwood Scrubs, depicting a lot of scrubbing worms, and Llanfairpwllgwyngyllgogery-chwyrndrobwll-llantysiliogogogoch, the Welsh railway station with the longest name in the British Isles, for which he drew a speeding train, as long as the station's name, with its wheels disappearing into the far distance like an endless spool of unravelling spaghetti. Some of these commissions came through the Curwen Press, however it was Stuart Menzies who first introduced Bawden to Fortnum & Mason, as the Stuart Advertising Agency handled their account during the 1930s. These drawings were populated variously with a plethora of anthropomorphic birds, beasts, fishes and insects celebrating every aspect of Fortnum's world-wide trade in delicacies for the table, from private dinners and cocktail parties to the stocking of hunting lodges in Scotland and the succouring of invalids. This campaign, which was curtailed by the war, was revived in the 1950s through the agency of Colman, Prentis & Varley with an even more colourful cast of characters with particular emphasis on Christmas and Easter celebrations. Cats, chickens, reindeer and Father Christmases abound, adorning a wide variety of colourful promotional literature and

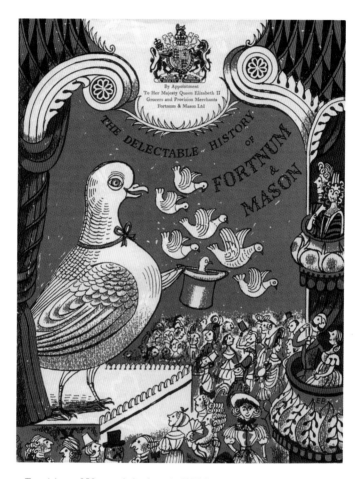

To celebrate 250 years in business in 1957, Fortnum & Mason's advertising agency Colman, Prentis & Varley commissioned Bawden to illustrate some of the characters and events linked to the firm, including visits by Indian Princes and windows in Piccadilly broken by Suffragettes.

ephemera. Today, all the materials Bawden designed for Fortnum's are collectors' pieces, especially *The Delectable History of Fortnum & Mason*, produced in 1957 to celebrate the firm's 250th anniversary.

Among Bawden's many strengths, which made his talent so much in demand with publishers and others, was his command of different media such as copper engraving, linocut, lithography and collage, which he would happily mix and adapt. However, he never allowed this flow of commissions to interfere with his career as a landscape painter, holding regular exhibitions of his distinctive watercolours in London at the St George's Gallery, Zwemmer's, the Leicester Galleries and later at The Fine Art Society. For the duration of the war it was this aspect of his work that became dominant. In 1940 he was commissioned as an official War Artist with the rank of captain, and during the next five years he was to work in Normandy, North Africa, the Middle East and Italy producing a wide range of highly esteemed watercolours, many of which are in the permanent collection of the Imperial War Museum. A rare piece of design from this period, and in an unusual medium, is *Christmas Convoy*, the seasonal news sheet produced in 1942 on board the SS *Westerland*, the ship on which he was returning to Britain from New York. He had originally been returning to England four months previously aboard the SS *Laconia*, a transport ship, when it was torpedoed; lucky to be alive, he spent five days in an open boat before being rescued by a Vichy French ship and interned in Morocco. From there he was later liberated by advancing American troops and shipped off to Norfolk, Virginia, hence his presence on the *Westerland* that Christmas. With typical Bawdenesque humour, his illustrations to *Christmas Convoy*, which had to be produced on the office duplicator, included a title page depicting a British lion and an American eagle preparing to tuck in to a seasonal dish of turkey and sausages.

One design project that straddled both sides of the war was the Bardfield Wallpapers designed in conjunction with his Essex neighbour John Aldridge. Originally produced in 1938–9, they were hand-blocked by John Perry & Company and retailed through Muriel Rose's Little Gallery. Production, however, had been discontinued for the duration of the war and in 1946 the blocks were transferred to Cole's. The Bardfield Papers now became very much a part of post-war taste along with Ravilious Wedgwood china – especially

Travel — and furniture and textiles by Robin and Lucienne Day, Ernest Race, Marianne Straub, and other innovators whose style came to epitomise the Festival of Britain.

Once reinstalled at Brick House, his Great Bardfield home, and with a new large studio extension built at the rear, Bawden returned to design work with renewed vigour. Book illustration, advertising material, mural painting and print-making occupied much of his time for the next quarter of a century, with occasional digressions into designs for tapestries, textiles, ceramics and garden furniture. Murals became an important part of his *oeuvre*, starting in 1947 with the commission from Colin Anderson of the Orient Line for *English Garden Delights*, a decoration for the first class lounge of the RMS *Orcades*; this was followed a couple of years later by a further mural, *The English Pub*, to decorate its sister ship the *Oronsay*. Anderson also commissioned curtain fabrics for the *Oronsay* as well as the transfer-printed bone china tableware, *Heartsease*, specially manufactured by Wedgwood's. *Heartsease* is an ingeniously simple pattern in mauve and grey based on the flower and leaves of the pansy, from which it takes its name. It is designed in such a way as to allow for flexibility in its application to the different ceramic forms that make up the set: teacup and saucer, coffee cup, bowl, plates of different sizes and a muffin dish and lid. These, as well as the linen curtain- and wall-fabric that he designed for the Time-Life Building in New Bond Street, London, sit alongside the Bardfield Wallpapers as prime examples of the post-war aesthetic associated with both the Festival of Britain and the coronation two years later of the young Queen Elizabeth II.

Unlike his earlier murals, *English Garden Delights* and *The English Pub* were painted on panels in the new Brick House studio and only installed after completion. The nostalgic English theme they evoke was followed again in the 45ft high, seventy-one panel mural, *English Country Life*, painted for the Lion & Unicorn Pavilion at the Festival of Britain. Many of his favourite motifs recurred in this vast mural — East Anglian churches, country houses, cows and tractors — as well as images of crabs, prawns, pheasants, hares, cauliflowers, carrots and bowls of fruit, familiar from vignettes in pre-war Ambrose

An original line drawing, reproduced here at just under full size, for a tail piece in Ambrose Heath's *Good Food*, published by Faber & Faber, 1932.

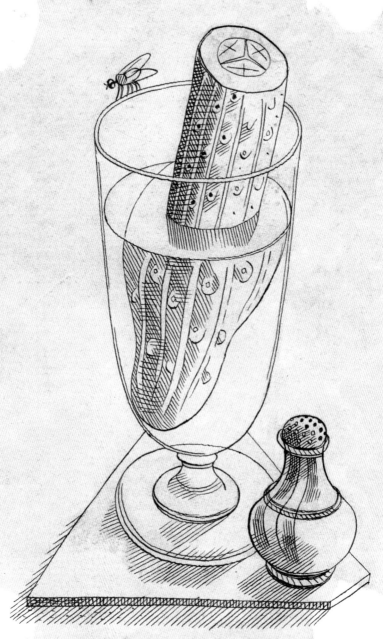

Heath cookbooks. Despite its great size, and designation as one of the most important art works created for the Festival, it was destroyed due to bureaucratic bungling, and is only known today through photographs and Bawden's beautiful small-scale model preserved along with his archive at The Higgins Art Gallery and Museum, Bedford. Bawden had a model-maker's delight in creating small-scale versions, which he made as much for his own pleasure as to show the client, who, in most cases, would have been satisfied with preparatory drawings and sketches. When designing the mural for the entrance hall to the Morgan Crucible Company building on the South Bank of the Thames at Battersea, now demolished, he inserted a detailed study into one of the architect's models.

Several of these post-war murals were for temporary structures, such as the British Pavilion at the Brussels International Exhibition (1958) and Expo '67 at Montreal; others were for seemingly more permanent sites, such as the Morgan Crucible building, the Physics Block at Hull University and Britannic House – the headquarters of BP. In preparation for the latter, a decorative design based on Saracenic architecture measuring over 12 feet in height and 30 feet in length – the largest mural he ever painted – BP sent him and his wife on a study trip to Isfahan. The fact that this again was painted on panels at Brick House rather than directly onto the wall, helped secure its preservation and it is now re-sited at the Chelsea and Westminster Hospital. The Principal of the rebuilt Morley College also commissioned several new murals including one by Bawden, this time representing scenes from Chaucer's *Canterbury Tales*; an appropriate subject as the College is situated on the original pilgrim route from Westminster.

Historically, tapestries have often been treated a bit like murals with the added advantage of being easily transportable. *Farming*, Bawden's 1950 design for the Dovecote Tapestry Studios in Edinburgh, echoes the agricultural theme of his other large-scale works of the period. However, in those days when war-time rationing was still in place, its imagery of nature's bounty – sheaths of corn, birds' eggs, cows and chickens, as well as a tail-less turkey reminiscent of Edward Lear's dodo – must have seemed to the public like the memory of a vanished Eden. The tapestry's border of patterned lozenges, like mediaeval masons' marks, is a typical Bawden device, the creation of pattern having been a part of his professional life since his days at the Curwen Press; for his later tapestry, *Bunyan's Dream*, which was embroidered rather than woven, he devised a geometrical border. *Bunyan's Dream*, commissioned in 1977 for the Cecil Higgins Art Gallery, Bedford, to mark the Queen's Silver Jubilee, was a remarkable collaboration between Bawden and members of the Bedfordshire Music and Arts Club, who embroidered the twenty individual panels: these were later stitched together at the Royal College of Needlework to make up the tapestry. Bedford was the birthplace of Bawden's hero, John Bunyan, and for his design he devised a grid that both formed the bars of Bunyan's prison cell as well as charting the progress of Pilgrim from the City of Destruction to the Celestial City: a conceit that not only works visually, but also facilitated the dividing up of the panels between the various embroiderers. He returned again to designing tapestries in 1984 when, following a visit to Egypt with his daughter Joanna, he produced half-a-dozen cartoons for the Dovecote Studios in Edinburgh. At the time discussions were held concerning the weaving of these, but for various reasons, mainly financial, the scheme lapsed. However, the project was revived in 2012, when two samples were woven as part of the Dovecote's centenary celebrations, and in the hope that a patron might finally come forward to commission one or all of the tapestries.

John Ward, who had been a student at the Royal College in the 1930s recalled a showcase outside one of the studios that Bawden filled with treasures found in the small town shop, noting that he 'revelled in the small change of Art.' It was this spirit that drove his interest in the minutiae of varied and different crafts; the commission for *Bunyan's Dream*, lead him to immerse himself in the study of wools and dyes and discussions about stitches per square inch. A few years earlier he had had to devise a decoration for Carrs Lane Congregational Church in Birmingham, depicting the three earlier chapels that had previously stood on the site. After much thought, and given the awkward positioning of the wall to be decorated, which was lit only by raking light from a side window, he created one of his most curious works, technically speaking. It is made up from pieces of linoleum, wood, nails and drawing pins – treasures of the small town shop – which must have evoked memories of the parental ironmongery in Braintree. His decision, however, to use nails as the major component was

An early watercolour design for the cast-iron *Bilston* garden seat, above, and final design, below, c1955. Made by Bilston Iron Foundaries, Robert Harling, who was working for the company's advertising agency, suggested the idea as a means to promoting the company.

practical not sentimental; a painting would have been hard to see in that position, while the shiny lacquered heads of the myriad of assorted nails pick up and reflect the light.

His war-time experiences in North Africa and the Middle East, the sights he had seen and the subjects he had drawn, were to stand him in good stead for the rest of his life. One of the first book covers he designed soon after his return to Bardfield was for Albert Camus's *The Outsider*, set in Algeria, and in 1947 he was commissioned to illustrate *The Arabs*, a Puffin Picture Book, which, once again, was printed at the Curwen Press. Apart from his familiarity with the topography of the region, his figure drawing had become firmer and more confident as a result of the portrait studies he had been obliged to make in his rôle as a War Artist: it was of particular advantage that his Arab sitters – whether sheikhs or peasants – did not speak English, and so he was under no pressure to make conversation and thus felt completely comfortable in their presence. *The Arabs* was followed a couple of years later by another slim volume – even after rationing ended, paper remained a scarce commodity – *Life in an English Village*. Noel Carrington wrote a broad-brush text for this King Penguin publication, but Bawden's illustrations are specific to Great Bardfield, with many identifiable personalities. It remains one of the most engaging vignettes of English village life, a last glimpse before so many time-honoured crafts and traditions were swept away and the motor car became ubiquitous, turning villages into dormitory suburbs, thus depleting them of butchers, bakers and other shops. Bawden's sense of humour, which had become more sardonic during the war years, found new targets, just as he found new champions, especially Robert Harling and Ruari McLean. Harling commissioned, among other things, a series of advertisements for the Zinc Development Association, which appeared in the *Architects' Journal* and *Architectural Review*, as well as getting him to design a cast-iron garden seat for the Bilston Foundry. Commissions during these years came from many sources, the BBC, the British Council and London Transport among them. He drew the light-hearted cover for the *BBC Year Book 1947*, with its plethora of fairies – male and female – playing musical instruments as they float down Portland Place, he designed posters for Ealing Studios, beer bottle labels for Walker's and beer mats and match folders for Gilbey's, as well as coronation decorations for Selfridges store in Oxford Street.

The 1950s and '60s were to witness the production of his most ambitious linocuts: *Brighton Pier, Liverpool Street Station, The Blue Tractor, Lindsell Church,* his two Kew Gardens subjects – *The Palm House* and *Pagoda* – and the series of London Markets, the latter transcribed for lithography by Stanley Jones at the recently established Curwen Studios. Jones also transcribed his large 1985 wall-map, created for the exhibition, *Style of Empire, 1877–1947,* at Florida's Miami-Dade Community College; lithographic copies were presented to attendees at the private view. Since that spontaneous 1920s linocut of a cow, Bawden had become adept at 'doodling' in the medium, exploiting it to the full for his 1961 poster design, *York Races,* commissioned by Ruari McLean for British Railways, in which a few small individual cuts of figures and horses, printed again and again and variously coloured, enabled him to create an impression of both the crowd and the race. Linocut was a medium he frequently chose for its textural effect, sometimes using it in combination with other media, as witness the dust-jackets for books as varied as Saul Bellow's *The Victim* (1948), Iris Murdoch's *The Flight from the Enchanter* and Louis MacNeice's *The Sixpence that Rolled Away* (both 1956). Most remarkably, in 1982, at the age of seventy-nine, he chose to illustrate The Folio Society's three-volume edition of Mallory's *Chronicles of King Arthur* with seventy-one separate black on white linocuts, in which, as he said, he delighted in putting 'all the bloody bits which Burne-Jones left out.' Few artists could achieve such intensity and liveliness of design from so restricted a medium. Five years later, working for the same publishers, he again demonstrated that less can be more, with his large-scale cuts for *The Hound of the Baskervilles.* In 1989, the year he died, he made one last large print, *Our Family,* for the National Art Collections Fund, depicting a frog and attendant tadpoles; when he showed me one of his first proofs of this print, he had inscribed it 'No need for birth control'. Although now eighty-six, and failing in strength, his inventiveness and pawky humour remained as sharp as ever.

Peyton Skipwith

Lithographed illustration from separated linocuts for *The Sixpence that Rolled Away* by Louis MacNeice, published by Faber & Faber, 1956. (Tin toy collectors will know the aeroplane was made by the Gunterman Toy Company.)

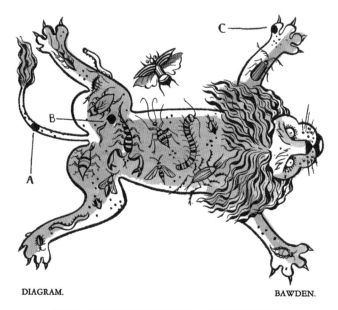

DIAGRAM.   BAWDEN.

OUT OF THE STRONG—SWEETNESS.

An ironic illustration to a grisly article in *Gallimaufry*, 1925, describing an African lion hunt during the First World War. The lion's skin, collected after the war had been eaten by insects. Bawden takes delight in drawing the author (see page 4) with a pop-gun, and labelling the splayed lion's minor injuries from an attack by a *Microgaster Baudenius*, described by the editor as 'a specimen which had hitherto escaped the attention of all but the most searching entomologist'.

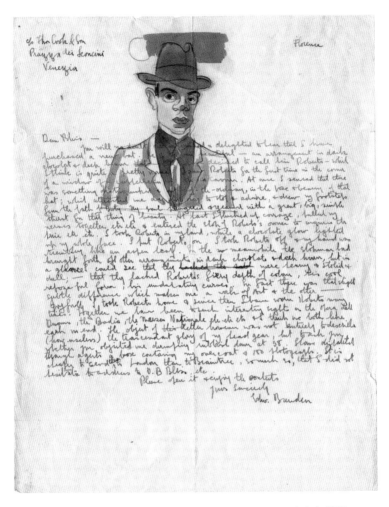

Bawden won the Royal College of Art travelling scholarship to Italy in 1925 (Ravilious had won it the previous year). In this letter to Douglas Percy Bliss from Florence, he rapturously describes the purchase of a 'dark chocolate and deep brown' hat, which he named 'Roberto' and illustrated in a self-portrait.

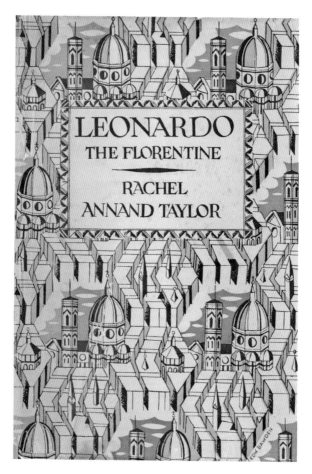

Leonardo the Florentine by Rachel Annand Taylor, described as
'a study in personality', published by the Richards Press, 1927. Also
from 1927, opposite, a proof lithograph printed at Curwen Press
of what appears to be an unused design for the Westminster Bank.

MR. WILKINS TAKES A BIRD'S-EYE VIEW OF BRANDLEGUARP

Colour stencilled illustrations, above and opposite, from Robert Paltock's novel of the adventures and imaginary voyage *The Life & Adventures of Peter Wilkins*, Edward Bawden's first illustrated book, published in 1928 by Dent, London and Dutton, New York.

KING GEORIGETTI'S RITELIA

MR. WILKINS BUILDS A LARGE TENT WITH THE HELP OF HIS TWO SONS

ABOVE AND BELOW

BREAK OF DAY

GAIETY AND GHOSTS

Opposite, the title page and above, chapter headings for
East Coasting, by Dell Leigh, published by the London and
North Eastern Railway, 1930. Printed by Curwen Press.

Ceramic tiles produced throughout the 1930s after designs by Bawden for Poole Potteries, opposite, and a map of the town, the centre spread from *Pottery Making at Poole*, above, 1925, commissioned by Harold Stabler while Bawden was still a student at the Royal College of Art and printed by Harold Curwen at the Curwen Press.

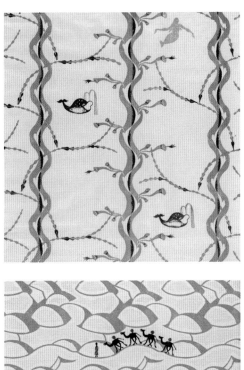

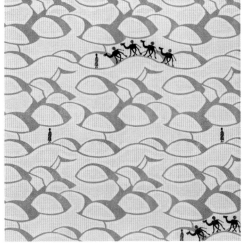

Opposite, one of Bawden's first linocutting experiments as a student, c1924. The pattern became the *Tree and Cow* Curwen wallpaper, in 1927. Altogether, he designed half a dozen patterns, including *Mermaid and Whale* and *Sahara*, above, during the 1920s.

In 1932 Curwen commissioned four designs as part of the *Plaistow Wallpaper* range (named after the location of their printing works in east London), including *Façade*, opposite. Later, in 1939 Bawden and his friend and fellow Great Bardfield resident John Aldridge embarked on printing wallpapers themselves. *Capital* and *Base*, above and below, closely related to Bawden's *Flute*, did not get into production, interupted by the war.

Headpieces for C.B. Cochran's compilation *Review of Revues.*

Printed at Curwen Press and published by Jonathon Cape, 1930.

Cover and headpiece for *The Choice of a Shipping Agent.*

THE CHOICE OF A
SHIPPING AGENT

Over two hundred years ago Sir George Saville reminded
us that 'We are in an island, confined to it by God
Almighty, not as a Penalty but a Grace, and one of the
greatest that can be given to Mankind. Happy confine-
ment, that hath made us Free, Rich and Quiet; a fair
Portion in this World, and very well worth the preserv-
ing; a Figure that ever hath been envied, and could
never be imitated by our Neighbours.' True as these

3

Printed at Curwen Press for Thomas Meadows & Co, 1931.

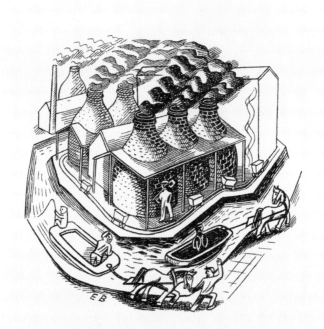

STOKE·ON·TRENT

BUT

SHELL ON THE ROAD

The 'You can be sure of Shell' advertising campaign ran from 1932.
John Betjeman wrote the words and Bawden drew the pictures.

As well as *Stoke-on-Trent* and *Gerrard's Cross*, the series included *Ashby-de-la-Zouch*, but *Shell sur la route* for bi-lingual readers.

Well on the Road by Christopher Bradby, published by G. Bell and Sons, 1935.
Bawden's jacket illustration is from a series of linocuts and the story illustrated
by line drawings from Shell advertisements ... by permission of Shell Mex.

FRINTON-ON-SEA

LITTLESTONE-ON-SEA

LLANTEGLOS-BY-FOWEY

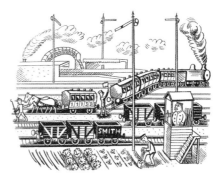

ASHBY-DE-LA-ZOUCH

STRATFORD-ON-AVON

(The birth-place, living-place, and death-place of
William Shakespeare)

LEE-ON-THE-SOLENT

The visit to Tunbridge Wells by the young Princess
Victoria in 1822, celebrated on the lid of a biscuit tin
for A. Romary & Co (of Tunbridge Wells), in 1934.

Shelf Appeal cover, January 1936. Matchbox, pub games, toothpaste tube with a smile, pencil and measuring tape for the 'monthly publication devoted to the planning, designing, manufacturing and display of the package'. Edward Bawden's linocut converted to lithography.

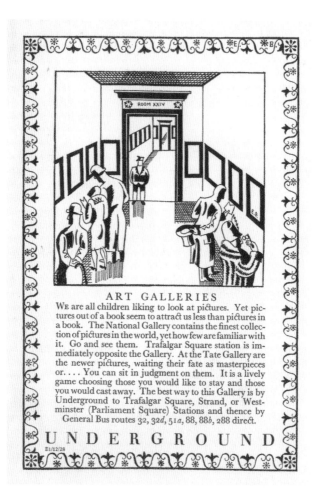

One of a series of press advertisements for the Underground, 1926. London Transport in its many forms was one of Bawden's long-standing clients, beginning while he was still at college he designed posters and advertising over a 25-year period for the company.

Chestnut Sunday, a 'windows bill' poster for London Transport, 1936, lithographed from a three-colour linocut. The 252 × 315mm poster was reproduced by Curwen Press as an inset illustration in *Signature* magazine to accompany an article on Bawden's printed work.

Bawden's relationship with Harold Curwen and Oliver
Simon lasted thoughout their working lives, the linocut
cover of *Curwen Press Newsletter 8*, above, featuring the
Curwen Unicorn, was cut in 1934. The copper engraving,
opposite, was produced as an experimental print to
accompany an article 'Graven Images, Line Engraving and
the Illustrated Book' by Graham Sutherland for *Signature* 6
magazine, 1937. Bawden had previously printed a series of
copper engravings in the 1920s.

A mocha jug, a wrought-iron garden bench and summer house from Bridge End Gardens, Saffron Walden. Bawden painted local images close at hand for the International Building Society Club, Park Lane, London, in 1938. When he went back to look after the war it had been overpainted in grey.

The Noah's Ark designs for Sheffield's City Library, commissioned in the 1960s, did not get past the design stage.

1934

1935

1937

1939

Bawden designed covers, title pages and illustrations for ten of Ambrose Heath's cookery books, published by Faber & Faber, from the first, *Good Food*, in 1932 to the suitably austere *Good Food without Meat* in 1940. The watercolour sketch design below for May from *Good Food*, depicts Eric Ravilious and Thomas Hennell on the left and Edward Bawden and Tirzah Ravilious on the right, in Brick House garden.

Sooner or later we shall need new stations ...

Sooner or later we shall need new docks ...

xxvi   JOURNAL OF THE ROYAL INSTITUTE OF BRITISH ARCHITECTS   *April* 1942

Sooner or later
we shall need new wharves...

New wharves, new loading depots new buildings of every kind will begin to arise in the year 194–. We will not hazard a guess at the exact date; it may be sooner than we expect. Early or late however, the post-war reconstruction will confront our architects and builders with the biggest job since 1666. What part will Zinc play in the new building programme? Its lightness, long life and essential cheapness seem to mark it out for a prominent part. More we do not claim.★ For the time being our object is just to suggest that you should

...keep ZINC in mind

We can claim, however, that Zinc has been used on the roofs of thousands of warehouses in practically every port of Britain! If you would like to know more about Zinc and the Zinc Development Association, write to the Z.D.A., 15 Turl Street, Oxford.

Sooner or later we shall need new wharves ... From the early years of World War II, the Zinc Development Association commissioned Bawden, while serving as an official War Artist, to draw their forward-looking advertising campaign, 1942.

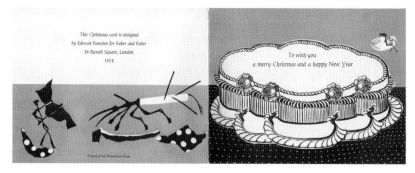

Top, *Old Crab and Young*, printed from a line block and hand coloured, a personal Christmas card from Edward and Charlotte Bawden, c1956. Above, a surreal greeting, including a matador fighting a fork, from Faber & Faber, 1952. Left, The *Titfield Thunderbolt* Christmas card produced for Ealing Studios in 1953.

Left and below, *Take the Broom* was one of six little books drawn in pen and watercolour for Edward Bawden's children in the 1940s. Not originally designed for publication, the double page spread below was drawn at a later stage to make up the right number of pages for printing.

The book was redrawn by Bawden and lithographed by Sheila Robinson, one of his students at the Royal College of Art, above and right, in an edition of 350 copies for George Rainbird and Ruari McLean in 1952. The series grew into *Hold Fast By Your Teeth*, published by Routledge and Kegan Paul, 1963.

Traveller's Verse. Gwyneth Lloyd Thomas, fellow of Girton College and an old friend of Charlotte Bawden, selected the anthology of poems.

Edward Bawden drew the 'on the plate' lithographs at
the Curwen Press, published by Frederick Muller, 1946.

A Few
General Hints

A few basic
recipes

Soups

Vegetables and
Salads

Cook Book Note-book, 'the result of many years' eating experience
in the continent and in America' by Magda Joicey, published by John
Westhouse, 1946. With surreal section divider illustrations by Bawden
and notes on each recipe by Miss Angela Carter, a 'dietetic expert'.

Also published in 1946 by John Westhouse, *Death and the Dreamer*, by Denis
Saurat, a novel in which the author states every detail is true. Suitably illustrated
with more surreal drawings by Bawden, it would appear the style of drawing for
both books was suggested by the publisher.

Design – Edward Bawden

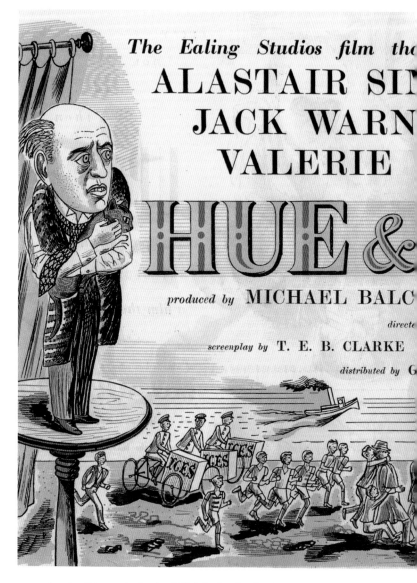

An advertising poster for the 1947 Ealing Studios film *Hue & Cry*.
Bawden recalled that for the design of the poster he was given
a completely free hand 'I worked completely in the dark – never

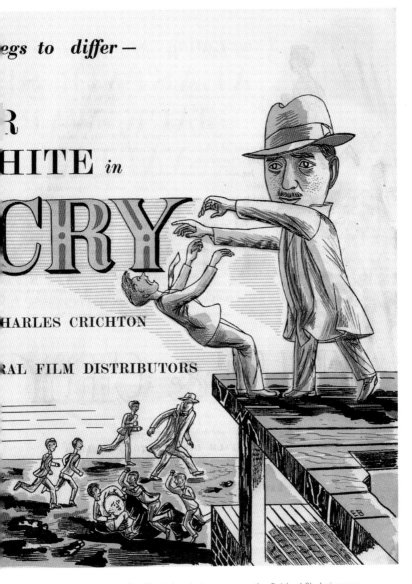

saw the film being shot, never saw the finished film', six years later Bawden was commissioned to design the posters and advertising for *The Titfield Thunderbolt*.

Full-page lithographed illustrations for *Gulliver's Travels, The Voyages of Lemuel Gulliver to Lilliput and Brobdingnag* by Dean (Jonathan) Swift, published by The Folio Society, 1948. Printed at the Chiswick Press, Bawden was re-commissioned to illustrate the book in 1965, this time printed by W.S. Cowell of Ipswich from their Plastocowell lithograph plates.

Life in an English Village, King Penguin, 1949. The village is Great Bardfield, Essex, the Bawdens' home for more than thirty years. Above, hand-coloured proofs from the black lithograph plates.

Final illustrations lithographed in six colours (the pipe smoker propping up the bar is the artist John Aldridge, neighbour and collaborator on the Bardfield wallpapers, 1939).

Above, one of a series of ceramic designs for the Orient line, 1952.
Below, a printed menu card designed to be overprinted on-board
ship, and an early design, right, 1950s.

Trial designs for Peter Walker Pale Ale bottle
labels, c1952, linocut and hand lettering.

VENTNOR

CHIPPING CAMPDEN

Illustrations from a series of leaflets to accompany British Transport films.

SOUTHWOLD

Alloway: Brig o' Doon

Printed by Westerham Press, 1954.

Horoscope beer mats for W.A. Gilbey Ltd, wine merchants and distilleries, c1954.

'The Signs You Drink Under', signs of the zodiac from
The Compleat Imbiber, published by W.A. Gilbey Ltd, 1954.

Cover illustrations for *The Twentieth Century* magazine, 1956.

Cover illustrations for *The Twentieth Century* magazine, 1955–58.

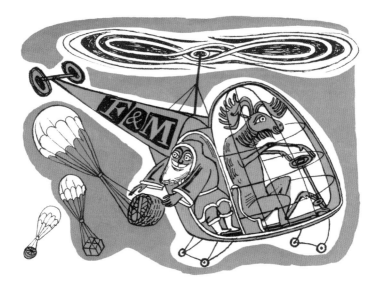

Edward Bawden designed some of his most entertaining illustrations for Fortnum & Mason in the 1930s. And in the 1950s, the advertising agency Colman, Prentis & Varley commissioned more: Christmas and Easter catalogues, leaflets and price lists.

ORDER TO

Christmas presents for friends abroad...
delivered by land, sea and air, 1957.

Easter catalogues for Fortnum & Mason Ltd. Above, *Fortnum's a-flutter for Easter*, left, *Brooding on Easter at Fortnum's*, and below, *Easter is early this year*, 1950s.

Before and after, Easter catalogue, Fortnum & Mason, 1950s.

Make life brighter, 1950s. A Fortnum & Mason A–Z.

Pierce the (winter) Gloom (with Fortnum & Mason), 1950s.

*Once upon a time there was a One Pound
Note and he married a Ten Shilling Note
and they had three children, a Half Crown
and a Shilling and a Sixpence and they lived
in a money box up on a mantelpiece.*

Louis MacNeice's children's story *The
Sixpence that Rolled Away* is generally
described as 'slight'. Bawden's illustrations
more than make up for cool literary reviews.
Published by Faber & Faber in 1956.

English as She Is Spoke, proof illustrations for the 1960 edition,
published by the Lion and Unicorn Press at the Royal College of Art,
lithographs from black line illustrations and ink-rollered colours.

The original, and sometimes hilarious *The New Guide of the Conversation in Portuguese and English* by Pedro Carolino was first published in 1883.

Faber & Faber, 1935

Dent, 1936

John Lehmann, 1948

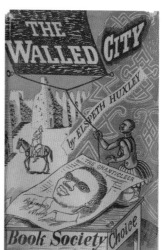

Chatto & Windus, 1948

Book jacket designs 1930s-40s

John Lehmann, 1949

Rupert Hart-Davis, 1950

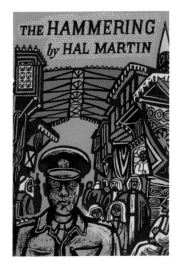

Faber & Faber, 1960

Faber & Faber, 1963

Book jacket designs 1940s-60s

Chatto & Windus, 1956.

Covers for the first edition of Iris Murdoch's *The Flight from the Enchanter*, published by Chatto & Windus, 1956 and paperback published by Penguin in 1962, above.

York Races, linocut, crayon and collage, opposite
and above, and early designs in pencil, pen and
watercolour, below, for a British Rail poster, 1961.

Linocuts transferred to ceramic tile panels for Tottenham Hale, above, and Highbury and Islington stations on the Victoria line Underground, c1968.

Linocuts from *The Morte D'Arthur*, Sir Thomas Malory's Chronicles of King Arthur, published in three volumes by The Folio Society, 1982.

Acknowledgements

The authors would like to thank:

Iris and Nigel Weaver

David Oelman and Gordon Cummings
at the Fry Art Gallery, Saffron Walden

Richard and Hattie Bawden

Tom Perrett and Victoria Partridge
at The Higgins, Bedford

Monica Grose-Hodge

Hannah Brignell
at Museums Sheffield

Andrea Tanner
at Fortnum & Mason

Traveller's Verse, 1941.